Hospitality

on a Wing and a Prayer

Entertaining without the pressure to be perfect

Beverly Graham Stickle

Pacific Press Publishing Association
Nampa, Idaho
Oshwa, Ontario, Canada

Edited by Kenneth R. Wade
Designed by Dennis Ferree
Cover and inside illustration by Sandy Nichols

Stickle, Beverly Graham, 1944-
    Hospitality on a wing and a prayer : entertaining without
the pressure to be perfect / Beverly Graham Stickle.
      p.   cm.
    ISBN 0-8163-1370-9 (pbk. : alk. paper)
    1. Hospitality—Religious aspects—Christianity. 2. Stickle,
Beverly Graham, 1944- . I. Title.
BV4647.H67S75 1997
177'.1—dc20   96-43770
                                          CIP

97 98 99 00 01 • 5 4 3 2 1

Contents

This book is dedicated to:

My husband, Don
- ◉ for dumping the strawberry shortcake, which gave me the idea for writing this book.
- ◉ for loving support and encouragement and
- ◉ for listening to all my tirades against the computer.
- ◉ Thank you for the many hours of help you gave.

My son, Ryan
- ◉ for his help, guidance, and patience in teaching me how to use the computer software.
- ◉ for answering his phone, quite often more than once an hour and walking me through my computer problems.
- ◉ Thank you for your kind and patient help.

My parents, Walter and Margaret Graham
- ◉ for teaching me about hospitality. Our home was always full of guests. Thank you for always being there for me.

Acknowledgments

Special thanks to Marian Forschler for sharing her energy, time, and talents. Without her this book would not have been written. Thank you, Marian, for helping with the initial proofreading and editing, explaining different writing procedures, helping when I had problems with the computer, and sharing ideas and suggestions.

To my sister Cheryl Klym and brother Darrell Graham, who are not afraid to admit that they are related to me.

To Susan Sanborn for loaning me her printer when I had a deadline to meet.

To Donna Koehn, who said "Bev, write a book."

To Loni Fischer Mooers for proofreading my manuscript and helping me with the last-minute problems with the computer.

To Maylan Schurch for encouraging me to "get writing" and to submit the manuscript to the publisher.

To Pastor and Mrs. Bill Smith for hosting that first seminar on hospitality and for graciously sharing their home with us. To my editor Ken Wade for wade-ing through the manuscript and bringing order out of chaos.

To the many women who shared their hints, secrets, and stories. The list includes: Kim Bryan, Lori Chinn, Charlene Davis, Rosemary Farver, Carolyn Firnkosis, Loni Fischer Mooers, Marian Forschler, Lorraine Fullbright, Stella Greig, Margaret Graham, Maureen Graham, Quida Hanscom, Dianne Hartle, Ruthie Jacobsen, Clara Belle Jenson, Cheryl Klym, Donna Koehn, Jackie Moore, Taunda Reicke, Ruth Reinking, Irene Reynolds, Carol Rick, Susan Sanborn, Carol Smith, Marji Venden, Becky Weigley, Midge Wilson, Diane White, and Marilyn Wolcott.

To the many men who gave their ideas and stories for the chapter on Not for Women Only. Included in this list are: Ben Davis, Kerry Forschler, Darrell Graham, Walter Graham, Bill Jenson, Kelly Nelson, Harold Richards, Don Stickle, Ryan Stickle, and Lee Venden.

Bev Stickle is available for a limited number of speaking engagements and seminars. For information, contact her through:
Her E-mail addresses:
76142.3100@Compuserve.com
or BevGrahamStickle@Juno.com
or Pacific Press Publishing Association
PO Box 5353
Nampa, ID 83653-5353

I'd Ask You Home, but . . .

I looked around the church
And spotted you.
I'd like to ask you home,
But what can I do?

There is a problem,
I must confess.
However you say it,
My house is a mess.

I have a can of beans
And five-minute rice.
If you were already my friend,
I wouldn't think twice.

But you are new,
What would you think
If you saw
Dirty dishes in my sink?

So I'll let you have
A lonely day.
Because I let
Pride stand in my way.

(If this is you, read on.)

CHAPTER ONE

Needed: A Wing or Wings

(to Fly Away When a Hospitality Disaster Strikes)

As the strawberry shortcake, whipped cream included, slid into Mary's lap, I gasped in horror. And I wasn't the only one. All nine guests gasped too. We couldn't believe what we were seeing. Don, my husband, had just dumped the dessert onto the dress of one of our guests.

I didn't know whether to commit a murder, run out the back door, or pray for a hole to suddenly appear in the floor into which I could disappear. How I wished for wings so I could fly away.

It took a moment or two, but sanity returned, and I quickly grabbed some paper towels. Between Mary and me, we managed to scoop up a large bit of the cake and strawberries. However, strawberry juice and whipped cream were quickly seeping into her dress.

I murmured, "I'm so sorry; I'm so sorry. We'll either pay for cleaning or for replacing the dress."

"Don't worry, dear," she said. I showed her where the bathroom was and left her to repair her dress.

Now, if I had been thinking kindly thoughts, I would have said to my husband, "That's OK, dear. Accidents happen. I appreciate your help." However, my thoughts weren't very kind and certainly couldn't have been uttered in front of our guests.

Years later, Mary and I laughed about the strawberry mess and realized that that incident had helped to cement our relationship.

My friend Jane says she, too, has wished for a wing to fly away. The beautifully decorated ice-cream cake just had to be cut. Her eight guests planned to attend a meeting and couldn't wait for the cake to thaw enough to be cut easily. Even her largest and sharpest knife wouldn't cut through the top layer. What was she to do? She used what she had.

After cleaning and disinfecting a small carpenter's hand saw, and in front of her guests, she sawed the cake. Jane said that everyone had a good laugh and enjoyed the dessert.

In another incident, Grandma made tarts for dessert. She placed one tart on the plate for everyone at the table. First, she served the bachelor beside her.

"Thank you very much," he said, as he took the plate, set it down in front of him, and ate all the tarts.

Long ago hosts had problems too

How humiliating! How could it have happened? What had gone wrong? They had correctly planned for the number of guests. Perhaps the extra-hot weather had made people more thirsty. However, the worst happened. They ran out of liquid refreshments. Then Jesus performed a miracle. The wedding coordinator tasted the new wine and pronounced it better than what had been served first (John 2:1-10).

In this, His first recorded miracle, Jesus turned a hospitality disaster into a blessing. He gave a lesson to all future Christian hostesses—don't panic, use what you have; you can survive any hospitality disaster.

There was also a lesson for guests—help, if you can and accept what you find.

Prayer for when a hospitality disaster strikes:
Dear Lord, I don't have wings to fly away,
so please turn this disaster into a blessing.

CHAPTER TWO

Now You Can Be Yourself

$\mathscr{E}$ven if you are too poor, too pooped, or too pushed, you can be yourself and be hospitable. Whether you are a career woman, a stay-at-home mother, a housewife, a working single mom, a handicapped woman, or a widow, Jesus loves you and accepts you where you are. So you can say, "This is where I am," and determine what you can do in your current position. I have personally had to make adjustments to my workload since being diagnosed with two different energy-sapping chronic illnesses.

If you stress yourself out by trying to do something that doesn't fit your energy, finances, personality, or time, you will end up not wanting to be hospitable again. So you need to find what fits your situation and do it.

If you want to be an elegant hostess and are in a position to do so, then be an elegant hostess. If you are struggling along in the survival mode, be a survival hostess.

If you have a lot of "shoulds" in your life, you will be very frustrated. It doesn't matter if you or somebody else put them there (husband, mother, church); they will drag your spirit down.

At times we may feel that we should be doing something—for example, having people over for dinner—when that may not fit our personality and situation. There are many other ways of being hospitable. However, if all you can do is smile at church (when you'd really like to kick the world), smile at church. Jesus loves you the way you are.

This is especially true for ministers' wives. Sometimes we put extra burdens on them, or they have too high expectations of themselves. But they are human too. It shouldn't come as a great shock to us that the minister's wife has as much right to be herself as the rest of us.

To get over feeling guilty, we need to make some of our "shoulds" into "coulds" and let the rest go.

I used to feel guilty when a speaker at church (usually a man!) said we should be hospitable. It made me feel like standing up and throwing a hymnal at him. I knew that if I tried, with my limited energy, to be an elegant hostess, I would end up elegantly dead.

Then I reread the story of Jesus' visit to Mary and Martha.

" 'Martha, Martha ,' " the Lord answered, " 'you are worried and upset about many things, but only one thing is needed. Mary has chosen what is better, and it will not be taken away from her' " (Luke 10:41, 42, NIV).

Jesus made two statements:

1. Martha, you are worried about many things.
2. Mary has chosen what is better.

Might He have been saying to Martha and to all hostesses:

⊚ I want you to be comfortable as a hostess.
⊚ I'd rather have a plainer meal and your friendship than a fancy meal and not visit with you.
⊚ I'm glad you baby-sat for the widow next door yesterday instead of spending all your time preparing a tidy house and fancy meal.

Notice what Jesus *didn't* say to Martha:

⊚ Mary is better than you.
⊚ Don't be such a perfectionist; you need to loosen up a little. The trouble with you perfectionists is that you either don't start something or don't finish it, because you always want it to be perfect.
⊚ You knew I was coming and had all week to prepare.

Why aren't you ready? You at least could have had an entree prepared and in the freezer!

◉ If you'd organize your time and life better, it would be easier for you to have company.

◉ If you were doing what a real Christian should, your house and meals would be examples to all who come into your home.

And what He *didn't* say to Mary:

◉ You lazy, good-for-nothing girl, get off your backside and help your sister!

Christ did not assign guilt!

It would be nice if we could always be ready for company, always have an extra entree in the freezer, always have a picture-perfect house. If you are at that place in your life, great!

I believe that Jesus wants me to be comfortable with whatever type of hospitality I choose. Jesus came to show me God's love and wants me to show this love to others. I can't show this love if I am miserably trying to do something that doesn't fit me.

When I recognize what I have in terms of energy, time, money, and personality, then I can better choose what type of hospitality will work best for me.

Prayer for hospitality:
Lord, please help me choose the type of hospitality
that best fits my personality, health, finances, and time.

Filling out the following personal data sheet will help you decide what will work for you. It can also be a guideline to help you know how to respond to things you read or hear others say. You will be able to say, "That may work for me. I'll try it." Or you might say, "At this time, I can't do it, and I'm not going to feel guilty." For example, if you are on a limited budget, you might make something for someone rather than buying something. If you have a physical disability, you might have to choose a type of hospitality you can do from your home or get someone else to work on the project with you. If, after filling in the sheets, you realize you are really overwhelmed during or after church, you may decide to have guests over for a meal at another time. If you are single, you might ask a friend to help you.

Personal Data Sheet

I have adapted this sheet from a form I use in seminars that I give on survival, called "Take 15." (Feel free to copy for personal use.)

1. Age: _____

2. Marital status:
_____ single
_____ married
_____ divorced
_____ widowed

3. Dependents (those people living with me or needing some of my time), their ages, any special needs such as wheelchair, diabetic, diet, etc.:

_____

_____

_____

_____

4. Live in:
_____ apartment under 700 sq. ft.
_____ house/apartment under 1000 sq. ft. with no yard
_____ house/apartment under 1000 sq. ft. with yard

____ house/apartment over 1000 sq. ft. with no yard
____ house/apartment over 1000 sq. ft. with yard

5. Money:
____ can buy whatever I want at any time
____ can buy what I want on payday
____ need to save for anything extra
____ always playing musical bills (the ones that land on the top of the pile get paid first). No extras for me.

6. Working (Women are always working! However, this means working for pay.):
____ Outside the home: hours away from home
____ Days off
____ Inside the home: hours needed to work

7. Organizations I belong to (church, social, work-related, etc.); when they meet, any special duties I have:

_____

_____

_____

_____

8. Pets—any special needs:

_____

_____

9. Energy level:
_____ I can do anything, anytime.
_____ I sometimes get tired but usually have enough energy to do what I want.
_____ I'm always tired.
_____ Any physical limitations: _____

_____

10. Talents:
What am I good at? _____

_____

What would I like to learn? _____

_____

11. List priorities in order of importance to you (God, health, husband, children, parents, work, etc.):

_____

_____

_____

12. Support system (with skin on—husband, parents, siblings, friends, church family):

_____

_____

13. Personality:

_____ I like everything to be spelled out to the last detail and done in a specific order.

_____ I like to have a few guidelines—sometimes spelled out, sometimes not.

_____ I like to do my own thing—make my own guidelines and do whatever needs to be done in any order that will get it done.

_____ I am so high-strung I could be a trapeze artist in a circus.

_____ I am so laid-back that a train could run over me and I wouldn't notice.

_____ I am really fussy about some things; other things don't bother me.

14. How I relate to God in making decisions:

_____ I'm always trying to run ahead of God. I make decisions and then pray for God to bless them.

_____ I expect God will answer my prayers by dropping something from heaven. Since He doesn't always work that way, I hardly ever make a decision but just let things happen.

_____ I methodically gather all the information I can get, pray about it, and then make a decision.

_____ I have to be poked with a cattle prod even to think about a problem, never mind pray about it.

15. I work best by:
_____ using index cards
_____ making lists
_____ making a schedule
_____ just doing whatever comes up during the day or what I feel needs doing
_____ Life is a bowl of cherries, and I haven't found a rotten one yet, so why work?

15. What does hospitality mean to me? _____

_____

_____

16. Check the reasons you are not more hospitable:
_____ I don't have time.
_____ I don't have money.
_____ My house is too small.
_____ I don't like having people in my home.
_____ Someone in my family doesn't like having company.
_____ My house is never clean enough.
_____ I can't cook fancy meals.
_____ I once had guests and made such a fool of myself I'll never have anyone over again.

CHAPTER THREE

That Better Part

Before we decide what we can do to be hospitable and how to do it, maybe we need to ask, what was the "better part" of hospitality Jesus spoke to Martha about?

What was Mary doing? She was sitting and listening to her guest. She gave Him the courtesy of her attention. She didn't rush about polishing the silver, folding the napkins, or lighting the candles. She was not making a gourmet salad dressing.

Did Jesus say there was anything wrong with polishing the silver, folding the napkins, lighting the candles, or making gourmet salad dressing? No. He said there was something better. He might be saying it is OK to do these things, but if you have to make a choice, choose what is better.

Martha "worried about many things."

Mary took care of her guest.

In the first hospitality seminar I attended, the speaker stressed that hospitality means caring about people, while entertaining means caring about things.

Could people, not things, be the better part?

Could Jesus have been saying, "Invite visitors over and serve macaroni and cheese or five-minute rice rather than rushing around preparing an elaborate meal; invite guests home, even if you haven't vacuumed or dusted"?

Could the better part sometimes be:

- Taking an elderly neighbor to the doctor's office during the week instead of making an entree for after church?
- Spending the money to pay for baby-sitting for a single mom rather than paying for the ingredients for an elaborate dessert to impress our dinner guests?
- Washing the invalid's floor instead of my own?
- Calling someone I missed at church instead of scrubbing the tub?
- Buying flowers for someone who is discouraged instead of for my own table centerpiece?
- Spending an evening doing something fun with my family instead of cleaning my home?
- Using my best dishes for my family on special nights and using whatever is quickest when we have guests (paper plates, paper cups, plastic silverware) so the hostess can relax?
- Sometimes serving food from the stove when we have

company so the hostess can join in all the afternoon activities too?

Prayer: Lord help me to choose that better part.

CHAPTER FOUR

Quick, Hide the Dishes

The preacher leaned over and whispered to Marlene, his wife, "Dear, we absolutely must invite home the two guest speakers and their wives. There's still two hours until the afternoon meeting."

"We can't!" wailed Marlene. "You know our house looks like disaster city!"

Marlene's grandma, who was sitting beside her, reached over and patted her granddaughter on the arm. "Never mind, dear; I'll help you. Just tell him to give us fifteen minutes."

When they arrived home, the grandma ordered, "I'll take the kitchen. You take the rest of the house."

Marlene dashed from room to room. She gathered up dirty towels, threw clothes into closets, pulled covers over beds, and put garbage into a bag.

Ding-dong, ding-dong, the doorbell pealed out the warning. Her husband had arrived with their guests. On her way to open the door, she glanced into the kitchen.

Spotless. *Grandma worked quickly*, she thought. She graciously welcomed her guests into her living room. The day grew hot. "Excuse me, I'll make some lemonade."

"Let us help," the two women guests said, following their hostess and her grandmother into the kitchen. After the lemonade had been made, one of the visitors asked, "Where do you want these peelings put?"

"Under the sink, please," the hostess said automatically.

The helpful woman opened the door under the sink. Three mouths dropped open. Three pairs of eyes blinked wide. Three pairs of eyebrows arched up. Silence. They saw dirty dishes stacked in piles—dishes from breakfast and yesterday's cooking and supper. Now the pastor's wife knew what Grandma had done with the dirty dishes.

Grandma broke the horrified silence. "That's OK, I usually put them in the oven!"

Everyone laughed.

What can we do if someone drops in unexpectedly and our house is a mess (not just needs vacuuming and dusting)? I strongly disagree with those who say to just ignore it and your visitors will too. In the first place, if their eyesight is good, they will see how untidy it is. Second, it could be really dangerous. If we all have our noses in the air trying to ignore the disorder, someone is sure to trip over something on the floor and break a leg. We could say (and I know someone who does—

I won't tell who), "I'm really glad you are here. If your life insurance and tetanus shots are up-to-date and you have a hard hat on, come in." We could say, "Enter at your own risk." We could get our visitors involved. "I'm in the process of (whatever you are doing or it looks like you should be doing). Do you have any suggestions?"

My friend Heidi told me about the time company surprised her. The doorbell chimed. There stood her friends. She had not seen them for a while. The only room at that time that had enough furniture to accommodate everyone was the family room. Sorted dirty laundry lay on couch, chairs, and floor. She said, "We are doing our weekly laundry." She brushed aside some of the clothes and told her company to have a seat.

The next time those people came to visit, the husband laughed and said, "The last time we were here, you were doing your laundry."

Would it have been better for her to ignore the mess or to say, "We are doing our laundry." And what if she needed to give a warning: "Careful, don't get your foot tangled in that bra!"

It's not just an idle concern—I once had someone trip on my laundry. The clothes were sorted into piles on the floor when a friend came by to work on plans for a women's meeting. My friend's six-year-old daughter went exploring and fell on a pile of clothes in a doorway. I didn't feel too bad though. She landed on the pile and wasn't hurt.

Besides, I figured she had it coming. Earlier she had spotted a little toy sewing machine on our bookcase and asked,

"Can I play with it?"

"Oh no, dear," I answered. "It was mine when I was a little girl. It's as old as I am and might fall apart if you touch it."

She looked at me, then at the sewing machine, then at me, then at the sewing machine again and asked, "Is it an antique?"

So I figured it served her right to fall on the laundry! It did teach me, however, to warn people to watch their step when I am doing the washing.

Your reaction to someone coming when the house is a mess depends on who is at the door:

- A friend? He or she will accept you the way you are.
- Your husband's boss? You might have to plan on divorce.
- Your boss? Plan on getting another job.
- A stranger? Who cares what the stranger thinks.
- Jesus? He loves you no matter what your house looks like!

Even when you think you have cleaned thoroughly and have everything under control, you may get a surprise. Ann felt great. Her apartment, though small, was neat and clean. She and her husband had most of the food prepared for her guests.

As Ann put the finishing touches on the meal, she heard the visiting husband ask, "What are these, Ann?"

She looked up to see the visitor dangling a pair of her

underwear in the air. Shocked and embarrassed, Ann stammered, "I usually fold the laundry on the couch!"

"Sure, sure," her guest teased.

Ann says "Although I almost died, that couple are now best friends with my husband and me."

It might be a good idea to take a quick glance around before you offer spur-of-the-moment hospitality. Grandpa's neighbor, Bob, had his car break down in front of Grandpa's house.

"Go right in and use the phone, Grandpa invited. It's on the wall in the hall."

As Bob walked toward the phone, he sidestepped. After he dialed the number, he moved as far as the cord would stretch. Then Grandma noticed the chamber pot, full to the brim and nearly overflowing, directly under the phone. Someone had brought it downstairs and set it under the phone before going to empty it outside. (For those who don't know, a chamber pot is a pot used to save a trip outside in the middle of the night to use outdoor restroom facilities.) It became a family joke when preparing for company to say, "Remember to empty the chamber pot and put it away!"

Have you noticed how, if your living room is clean, your husband will bring your guests in the back door? We might need to reeducate our husbands. For some reason, most of the people coming to our home come to the back door. I'm thinking of putting up a sign. "Before you can get to the back door, you have to go through a snake pit!"

But I haven't gotten around to putting the sign up yet. One day, paper was strewn over the dining table and linen chest. Paper, dirty dishes, and groceries that had just been brought from the store sat on the kitchen countertops. A businessman knocked on the back door.

"You are welcome to come in," I invited. "The house is a mess. I'm writing a book. Come into the living room. You may sit on that chair," I said, pointing to the only seat that was not covered with magazines and papers.

Our guest opted to stand; he probably thought it was safer.

Later, as he went out the door, he said, "Good luck on your book."

I wouldn't have been surprised if he had said to himself, "That's one excuse for a messy house I haven't heard before."

When I was moaning about that encounter to a friend, she said, "What are you worried about? You probably will never see him again." Thank God for a good friend who helps to keep things in perspective.

Has anyone ever come to the end of their life and said, "I wish I had cleaned more"?

When I'm old and rocking in my rocking chair, I want to think about people I've met and places I've been, not how many times I've scrubbed my floor.

Prayer for a dirty house:
Lord, please put blinders on my guests.

The Fifteen-Minute Checklist

What to do if you have only fifteen minutes to prepare for company. (It doesn't matter whether they have just called or you knew they were coming but had priorities other than cleaning!)

1. Living room and/or family room

Grab a large box or garbage bag and throw the mess into it.

Put the box or bag in a bedroom (the "Oh, No Room" my friend Betty calls it).

Tip: If the room is really cluttered, pick up only things that could be tripped over or sat on.

Warning 1: If there are important papers, put them in a separate place. (It took a friend three days to find papers she needed signed.)

Warning 2: If using a garbage bag, be sure not to place it where a family member will mistake it for garbage and throw it out. I am not going to tell you how I know about that one!

If you like the smell of furniture polish, pick the most visible piece of furniture or part of a piece; for example, the top of the coffee table. Then spray and wipe. The room will smell of furniture polish, and one piece will be shiny.

2. Bathroom

Gather the dirty towels; take one towel and quickly wipe the mirror, sink and counter, toilet lid, seat, and top of toilet bowl.

Close shower curtain or door.

Put out a clean towel. No clean towel? Try taking a dirty one and placing the other side out or putting out paper towels.

Make sure there is toilet paper on the roll.

Tip: Some guests like to look in medicine cabinets. Prepare for them. Set a mouse trap or a loud buzzer to go off when the door opens. (If that doesn't stop them, put in a live mouse.)

3. Bedrooms

Shut the door. Your guests are coming to see you, not tour your house. Make yourself feel better. Post a sign. Good possibilities include: Caution: Hazardous Waste; Caution: Toxic Waste; Death to All Who Enter Here!

4. Kitchen

Place dirty dishes in the dishwasher. No dishwasher, or dishwasher full? Don't panic. If leaving them on the counter or in the sink bothers you, or you are trying to impress your guests, hide them. Great hiding places include under the sink, in a cupboard, in the clothes dryer, or in the oven. One of my friends puts a tape across the oven control button as a warning—dishes in there. Taunda, who once forgot that the dishes were in there, likes the tape suggestion. Her parents were visiting, and she turned on the oven. When she started to smell something funny, she quickly turned it off again. Her folks were not aware anything was wrong. But she did have a burned and crusted mess to scrub off the dishes. If all these places are full or you need to use one of them, place the dirty dishes in a box or pan or whatever container is quickly available and place it in another room, out in the garage, in the car, or in a tub (only if you are absolutely sure that the bathroom won't be used—you might have to lock or block the door.) Depending on where you hid them and your mental state, you may need to write on the calendar where you put them.

But what if you're too tired to do any of this? Just do what you can do. Spend the fifteen minutes in bed or relaxing in a chair and SMILE when your guests arrive. They want you alive and not dead with a clean house!

Remember, your job is to be a warm and thoughtful hostess and not to make a big impression or make people think you or your house are great.

We all have different energy levels, time constraints, and personalities. One of us may need a perfect house. Another can live in a relaxed atmosphere. Some of us live in very, very relaxed atmospheres. Because our comfort levels differ, we must decide for ourselves what is best. At certain times in our lives, and depending on our personalities, we might plan to clean by using index cards, lists, or schedules. We might clean by: working an hour a day, doing particular chores on certain days, allotting a specific time slot once a week, or paying a cleaning lady. I don't presume to tell anyone else how to clean house. There are many books on how to organize housework. If you are organized, good. In this book I am not talking organization. I am talking survival.

If you're in the same survival mode or even if your organization has just been thrown off a little by emergencies, you may find the next section "Excuses for a Messy Home" useful!

Excuses for a Messy Home

There's no need to lie—after all, there probably is some project you're working on that has contributed to the mess. Here are some plausible possibilities:

If papers are strewn around: I'm doing my taxes; I'm sorting through my files; I'm writing a book.

If the kitchen is a mess: I'm cleaning my cupboards; I'm reorganizing my cupboards; I'm trying to see what dishes I have before I buy more.

If there are dirty clothes scattered around: I'm doing my laundry; I'm sorting clothes to give to the local charity; I'm packing for a trip.

One excuse never to use: I have a headache. The visitor might answer—or at least think—"Lady, if I had a mess like this, I'd have a headache too!"

Why Are Your Counters Clean?

The flip side of the excuses for having a messy house comes up when a house is suddenly "too clean." My friend Cheryl was delighted that company was coming, so she managed to get her kitchen countertops clean—a very rare phenomenon in her home. As she sat and visited with her guests, she noticed that one of the little boys she was babysitting was placing a toy on one of the counters.

"Please don't put anything on the counters, Paul," she said.

He looked and looked again, then asked, "Why are your counters clean, Cheryl?"

Here are some reasons why your counters might be clean:

1. You are very organized; maybe you should be writing this book.

2. Your mother or mother-in-law is coming to visit. (We won't look under your bed.)

3. The health department has threatened to shut down your kitchen. (Only ask them for an inspection when you need an excuse not to cook!)

4. Your husband always has to come home to a spotless house. One man quickly became my friend for life when he admitted that maybe he should clean the house himself.

5. You hid the dishes.

6. You spent time cleaning even though you might have been better off doing something for your health. (You might be cleaning for your health, either as a boost to your mental health or to prevent getting some weird disease from the little green things growing in the dish on the counter.)

7. You spent the time cleaning instead of enhancing a relationship when little Mary wanted you to watch the snow fall with her.

CHAPTER FIVE

Fifteen Minutes to Sanity

To keep your sanity, I suggest you forget what everybody else says to do. Think for yourself. List *your* cleaning priorities, not someone else's. All of us have two things that we must do to survive—dishes and laundry. If we don't do our dishes, we will either get sick from eating on dirty dishes or have to buy paper plates. If we don't wash our clothes, we'll either have to wear dirty clothes or go around naked. At times, some of us probably come pretty close to being both sick and naked. Therefore, washing dishes and laundry are two top priorities. However, how we do them can differ.

My friend Sarah overheard her five-year-old daughter. "Grandma, why are you hanging some clothes up and folding others? Mom just leaves them in a pile until we wear them."

When my nephew was little, the only person he had seen using an iron was his father, who ironed his own business shirts. One day my sister got out the iron to iron something, and my nephew asked, "Mommy, will daddy let you use his iron?"

To some people, making the bed is a priority. Others are lucky if they can find it. My friend Jane says she makes hers as a matter of survival. If she doesn't make it, she'll crawl back in.

You can say to yourself, "I can feel good about myself even if my house isn't clean or my bed made." You may feel better if it is cleaned. However, your value as a person is not associated with how your house looks. Any Christian who thinks otherwise better read the story of Mary and Martha again. If we get this idea into our heads, we will find it easier to cope. We might transfer this idea to loving others as Jesus did—with unconditional love.

Does this excuse us from all responsibility for trying to keep a clean house? No. But it does let us cope the best way we can, in whatever situation we find ourselves. If we can get organized, great. However, there will be times when we are barely surviving.

One way to survive is to break most cleaning chores (other than dishes or laundry) into fifteen-minute segments. Choose whatever you have listed as a priority for that day. Work on it for fifteen minutes. Don't work on it any more that day. Don't feel guilty. You've done your time. (I have had to clean this way for years. I set the timer for fifteen minutes. When the timer goes off, I stop. If I don't do this, I either land in bed or in the hospital.)

Fifteen-minute chunks

You may have to look at ways to clean differently. For example: to clean the kitchen, you may have been taught to do the dishes, wipe the counters, take out the garbage, and last scrub the floor. But if you always work in that order, you may never get to scrub the floor, and you may end up calling 911 to have the fire department come and pry you loose! Leave the dirty dishes, counters, and garbage. If garbage is on the floor, you will have to move it. Take fifteen minutes to scrub the floor.

If you need to leave dishes for one or more days and don't have a dishwasher, add one tablespoon of bleach to every gallon in your wash or rinse water. Once a week, or every couple of weeks, use this same solution to wipe down the kitchen counters. (Don't use it if bleach will damage the counters.) Use a plastic scratch pad to scrape off the dishes.

Some days it might take fifteen minutes just to make a path from the front door to the living-room couch. I am a "three swipes and you're out" person, so I prefer not to have a lot of knickknacks around. Some people get around this by using glass cabinets to keep from having to dust so often.

June, a friend, says she will pick a chore that she doesn't like, then take her cordless phone and call someone she thinks might need a phone call, and work on that chore while talking on the phone. What a great idea!

Fifteen-minute sanity-restorers

Here are some suggestions for breaking your work up into short segments that at least help you feel better about yourself and make a dent in the disarray:

1. Refrigerator

(My husband says that the refrigerator is a place to store food until you throw it out—I plead the fifth!)

- Clean one shelf.
- Clean inside the door or one shelf on the door.
- Wash the front. (My friend Molly says it would take her more than fifteen minutes to take everything off her refrigerator door. She may take two days to do the job.) If there are a lot of things on the front, maybe it won't get dirty so fast. How about using huge posters to cover the doors? Instead of cleaning the front, change posters.
- Clear and wash the top. Sue, a friend, says she only cleans the top of her refrigerator when "stuff" is sticking out so far she has to start ducking as she goes by.

2. Stove

- Clean the top or one part of the top.
- Wash the outside of the oven door.
- Spray the oven and inside the oven door with cleaner.
- Clean storage drawer under the oven.
- Wipe out the oven. (May take more than one fifteen-minute time slot.)

Tip: When you turn on an element on the stove and your smoke detector goes off, it is time to clean under that element.

3. Cupboards

◎ Clean one shelf. (For more than twenty years I have used linoleum or vinyl to line my kitchen and bathroom drawers and cupboards. I don't have to change it unless I want a different color.)

◎ Clean a drawer.

◎ Wash the front of the cupboards. (Or some of the cupboards.)

4. Vacuuming and dusting

◎ Vacuum and /or dust one room at a time. (It may be faster to vacuum or dust only as far as you can go in fifteen minutes.)

5. Bathroom

◎ Wipe mirror.

◎ Scrub sink and counter.

◎ Scrub toilet.

◎ Scrub tub. (This often gets left to last, so you might want to make it first sometimes.)

6. Bedroom

◎ Change sheets on bed and tidy night stand.

◎ Clean under the bed.

◎ Clean one drawer of the dresser.

◎ Clean the closet or part of the closet. (Some of our walk-in closets may be look-in closets because they are too full to be entered safely!)

7. General cleaning chores

◎ Washing light switches throughout house.

◎ Sorting through the box you threw into the bedroom when company was coming. (May only be able to get

through the first inch.)
◉ Filing just one or two inches of paper.
◉ Cleaning one set of blinds.

Now you are getting the idea. With all these jobs, some may take longer than one fifteen-minute time period. Sometimes two or more may be done in fifteen minutes. If you are cleaning something, for example, a closet that will take more than fifteen minutes, you may have to leave things out in another part of the room or house until you have time to finish the project. You don't want to spend fifteen minutes taking things out, then putting them back in the same place again. If you have small children and can't leave things out, you may need a larger time slot. Trade baby-sitting with a friend, or have the friend help you.

When you clean, you can do little things that will help you keep things cleaner. Some people like to buy pretty dividers or containers to keep things sorted in drawers. Kitchens and bathrooms need containers that won't get ruined if they get wet—old ice cube trays, small containers such as soft margarine bowls, and plastic cups. In drawers in other places, you can use less durable items, but you might want to cover them with contact paper or wallpaper to make them look nice. These are nice touches and can add zest to your day whenever you look at them. Possible things to make dividers from include tops or bottoms of boxes (cake or muffin mix boxes that have been cut down), stationery boxes, the little boxes checks are sent in, and jars from baby food. Here we are talking survival. Use what you have when you need it.

Remember, if you are in the survival mode, spend only fifteen minutes per day, and do only one chore. Feel good about what you have accomplished. Some days you may be too tired or too pushed to do any cleaning chores. You'll survive. Jesus loves you!

Prayer:
Lord, please help me:
to keep my sanity when my house is a mess,
to prioritize what job needs doing the most each day,
and not to criticize another when her house is a mess.

CHAPTER SIX

Beans Are Enough

*I*nvite visitors even if you plan on just opening a can of beans. Just make sure they are not too zesty. One day I served an unfamiliar brand of beans, then spent the night in agony, praying that my guests weren't in agony too. It turned out that I was the only one affected.

Frances, a new acquaintance, tells about one time when she and her family went camping. All week they were hot, dusty, and thirsty. She said, "We attended a church in the area. I was hoping someone would ask us home even for a can of beans and a glass of water. Nobody did."

"Would you have asked someone home to share a can of beans?" I asked.

"No," she replied.

Christina, one of my friends, asked someone to share

beans while in the middle of remodeling. Kitchen appliances sat in the middle of the room. The floor was stripped down to the boards, and dust and tools lay everywhere. She had spotted a woman and her family at church. She barely knew the woman, but said, "If you are not allergic to beans, would you like to come for dinner?"

"That person is now one of my best friends," she says. Christina adds that another time she used her best crystal and dishes, made a rose centerpiece (in February when roses are expensive), cooked a complicated casserole, baked an elaborate dessert, and invited a family with children. The wife thanked her for the lovely dinner but did not respond to her attempt at friendship. Christina said, "In retrospect, maybe I scared her off. She might have thought I do that all the time and she couldn't do the same."

When we think we have things well planned, the unexpected usually happens.

My friend Gerry told me, "Visitors we had one week still laugh about the time my husband, George, asked, "Honey, please throw me an apple."

Plop! Splatter! Chili on George's face. Chili down George's clothes. Chili on the tablecloth. Chili everywhere but in the bowl where the apple had landed.

Another time my friend Connie asked twelve people over to celebrate a friend's birthday. Since she had invited them to come at 7:00 p.m., Connie thought they would have had their supper. She made crepes, planning to serve one and a half per person. Suddenly she noticed guests taking two or three. Her guests had come expecting supper. But she had planned a dessert. So they ran out of food.

"What did you do?" I asked.

"Nothing," she answered. "I didn't have any more ingredients, so we just visited. Everyone survived, though I am sure they went home hungry!"

Tip: When extending the invitation, if it's not for an entire meal, specify that it is just for dessert.

Tip: When there's a limited amount of food available, either give each person their allotment on a plate or warn them in the beginning how many pieces are available per person.

Was Mrs. Zacchaeus ready for Jesus? How do you think she felt? Do you think she moaned, "Oh no! I don't have a thing prepared!"

Jesus didn't warn her. He just called Zacchaeus out of the tree and said, "Hurry up! I'm going to your house today" (see Luke 19:5-7).

What lessons do you think Jesus taught hostesses by His instant appearance at Zacchaeus's home? Could He have been saying:

- I'll be happy with whatever you have.
- Don't spend hours cooking for Me.
- You don't need a complicated entree or dessert.
- Had I warned you ahead of time, you might have thought you had to cook something as fancy or fancier than Martha did last week.
- I'd be happy with a bowl of beans.

What do you think the following people might have served Jesus?

Mrs. Zacchaeus—something quick, but she probably had servants to help her.

Abraham—probably a feast. Abraham liked to kill the fatted calf (Genesis 18:1-8).

Widow of Zarephath—a biscuit (1 Kings 17:12-24).

Each of the above would have used whatever they had on hand. Twice Jesus served fish and bread. Simple. Fast. What He had available (Matt: 14:18-21; 15: 32-39). If Christ felt comfortable serving plain, simple food, why can't we?

We don't always need to have a salad, a dessert, and a protein dish at every meal. People are not going to starve or become malnourished based on one meal. They will survive if sometimes we don't have dessert, sometimes we don't have a salad (serve two vegetables instead), sometimes we don't have a protein dish. (It's pretty hard not to get *any* protein. Most food has some.)

Sometimes things happen to the food that we are not expecting. My friend Jill told me of the time she made a new recipe. She used a famous cookbook and made curry. She had never used curry before. She says she didn't know about the different strengths of curry. Most of the guests couldn't even finish half of what they had taken. The husband had three helpings. As Jill went into the kitchen to get the dessert, she heard the visiting husband ask her husband, "What are we having for dessert? More curry?"

Tip: When using a new recipe, it might be a good idea to have a lot of water or juice on hand!

I have a friend, a minister's wife, who really does not like to have people to her home. One week after church, she braved having guests. As she was serving the meal, she broke a drinking glass on top of a casserole. Thankfully, the guests had already been served. She survived.

We can live even if things don't turn out perfect.

What about decorations? Most of the women I have talked with say that by the time they get all the food on their table, there isn't any room for a centerpiece. It is more important to have guests over than to worry that you don't have a centerpiece. (My sister-in-law says her centerpiece is what holds the napkins.) If you have a centerpiece, how lovely. If you don't, don't worry. They are not necessary. For those limping along in the survival mode, you are lucky if you can have guests. If you feel you must have a centerpiece, use what you have on hand: something from a favorite collection, a souvenir from a trip, or a child's toy. For my son's fourth birthday party, I washed his large firetruck, put plastic wrap on it, and placed sandwiches in the truck. It was a big hit with the children.

It's especially important that you make entertaining easy enough so you feel comfortable doing it regularly. Stay within your budget. Prepare food that doesn't take all your time and energy. If you overspend in your time, money, or energy, you will not want to ask anyone to your home again.

"Come over for a "canned" dinner, I tell my friends. They

know the meal I serve will be from cans.

There is nothing wrong with a bowl of soup and buns after church. When it is shared with a guest, the angels sing.

Paper plates and cups are becoming more acceptable. If you have them and want to use them, do it. Anything to make your life easier. Buy them in bulk to save money.

Jesus loves you no matter what you serve! He loves you whether or not you can have people to your home for a meal!

Potluck it

Perhaps the ultimate in simplicity for the hostess is to invite families over to share a potluck. One person doesn't have all the expense or time in preparing the meal, and you can still have great fellowship as you taste each others' favorite recipes. Here are some variations on the potluck theme that can add new interest.

1. Have everyone bring whatever pizza fixin's they have and let people make their own pizzas. Of course, if everyone brings olives, there's going to be a lot of "olivey" pizzas. You can do the same with sandwich fixin's or haystacks.

2. "You're on your own meal"—you put out what you have—canned soups, packaged foods such as macaroni and cheese, or other pasta dishes. Your guests make what they want. This can be a lot of fun as guests may team up to make a dish. Don't use expensive ingredients. If you don't want to supply all the ingredients, tell guests, "This is an 'on your own meal.' Bring what you would like that is quick and easy to prepare."

3. Last-minute potluck—after church ask a friend to bring

whatever and join you for lunch. We did this last week with a friend. She said, "We are having spaghetti. Would you like to come and bring something to go with it?" I took strawberries and cream. We ate spaghetti, green beans, carrot sticks, and strawberries with cream. So what if once in awhile there are two squash dishes?

Hints for making inexpensive and quick meals

There are a number of ways that may help you make quick but inexpensive meals:

1. Buy breads or buns at outlet stores or on day-old racks in the stores.

2. If tomatoes are expensive and you are having haystacks or burritos, use salsa, canned whole tomatoes or dried tomatoes, or simply skip the tomatoes.

3. When lettuce is expensive, make carrot and/or celery sticks, coleslaw, or shredded carrot salad.

4. Serve sauces separately from pasta, rice, etc. Leftover sauce can be used in another dish. Guests with allergies might be able to eat rice but not what is in the sauce.

5. Desserts are not necessary. However, you can have fruit, ice cream, a package of cookies, candies, or nuts.

6. Buy frozen prepared foods such as lasagna, pizza, and manicotti.

7. Buy packaged foods like macaroni and cheese, five-minute rice, and noodles.

8. Plain old white rice will cook in twenty minutes. This is good to serve because many people with allergies can eat rice.

9. Bake or mash potatoes. Potatoes can be baked quickly in a microwave. If you have lots of potatoes, put half in the microwave and half in the oven at 400 degrees. Switch after fifteen minutes. In thirty minutes you can have at least twelve baked potatoes. Potatoes will cook quickly if they are cut small. Then you can serve mashed potatoes.

10. I buy instant gravy in a large tub instead of in little packages. Two tablespoons mixed with one cup of water makes one cup of gravy. One pound of the mix makes one gallon of gravy. You can add whatever additional seasonings you wish.

For those who always have a casserole in the freezer, great. These tips are for people who don't.

Menu Suggestions for Meals That Are Quick and Inexpensive and Can Be Served After Church

My goal for these meals is that they should be made from easily found ingredients, take less than thirty minutes to prepare, and cost less than fifteen dollars for the entire meal for eight people. The desserts are not given, but desserts mentioned in the previous section could be added without going beyond fifteen dollars.

1. Spaghetti with tomato sauce, garlic bread, lettuce salad, green beans.

2. Rice, beans (from cans), lettuce salad, chopped olives, chopped tomatoes (or salsa), and buns.

3. Noodles, mushroom sauce (canned soup or white sauce with canned mushrooms), garbanzo beans (from a can), carrot salad, peas, buns, or bread.

4. Baked potatoes, grated cheese (or hot cheese soup or

sauce), sour cream, chopped lettuce, tomatoes (or salsa), buns, or bread.

5. Haystacks: corn chips, beans (from cans), chopped lettuce, chopped tomatoes (or salsa), cheese. Don't worry about the order that haystacks are placed on the plate. Everyone seems to do it a little differently.

6. Vegetable soup (three cans chunky vegetable with two to three cans vegetarian vegetable), buns with cheese or peanut butter.

7. Mashed potatoes with gravy, lettuce salad, corn (canned or frozen), cottage cheese, and bread.

8. Flour tortillas, beans, cheese, lettuce, salsa.

9. Flour tortillas with cheese in the middle, folded over and placed under the broiler, vegetable tray.

10. Macaroni and cheese, broccoli or peas, lettuce salad, and buns.

The above menus can be made cheaper and more healthful by making your own beans and soups. However, they will take longer to prepare. Slow cookers are handy for soups, stews, beans, or chili for cooking after church. The plainer the food served, the less work it is for the hostess. Those people with dietary restrictions may appreciate it too.

Prayer:
Lord, please bless the food but, more importantly, help my guests to be fed with the food of friendship.

CHAPTER SEVEN

Sit on the Floor

Sit on the floor? You mean have guests over and have them sit on the floor? What did Jesus do? When it came time to feed the multitudes, did Jesus say, "Send them home; we have no tables, no chairs"? No. At least twice He used what there was. What did the people use for a table? The grass. What did they use for chairs? The grass.

Have you ever wanted to ask a family to your home and thought, *I can't because my furniture isn't good enough?* There have been times when I'm sure I missed a blessing because I wouldn't have someone to my home because I thought it wasn't good enough.

Once, however, when we had just moved into a new home, we had too many guests to fit around the kitchen table. We did not have any living-room furniture. We served the food from the kitchen table, and all sat on the living-room carpet. I put sheets and towels on the floor for tables. Everyone seemed to enjoy it.

Have you had the experience I have, where you'd visited in two different homes, both with lovely furniture—the decorations just so and the food superb—but you felt comfortable and enjoyed yourself in one home, while in the other home you spent the afternoon worrying that you or your children might break something? Or have you visited in two homes where things weren't so perfect? Maybe even a little messy. Did you feel comfortable in one home and uncomfortable in the other? What made the difference? Was it your surroundings or the people? As I look back on the homes I've visited, I know that the people are far more important than the furniture.

Don't despair if your furniture looks as though it has gone through a war. It probably has—your family's. Just call it memory furniture. Think of all the memories that have been made using it.

What can you do if it embarrasses you? Be creative. Use sheets, bedspreads, blankets, quilts, or afghans to cover couches or chairs in the living room. Cover a sheet of plywood with a tablecloth or a sheet to make a table.

Don't compare your home to someone else's. There will always be someone who has more and better furniture or a fancier home. However, remember there will also be others who don't have what you do.

Your success as a hostess is not based on what you have but on what you are. If you are warm and friendly, your guests will have a good time.

Tip: It is not your furniture or how your house looks but how you accept your guests and how they feel that acceptance that counts.

If you want to have more people over than you have chairs, you can have some guests sit on the floor or ask some to bring chairs. If you know ahead of time that some people might have to sit on the floor, be sure to tell them. The main advantage of having a lot of people at one time is that the more people, the less likely they will be to notice any dust in the corners. You may also decide that it is easier to have more people at one time than somebody every week. However, the best way to get to know people is to have only a few over at one time.

Elaine, a friend, says that when she has a number of children as guests, she always puts a tablecloth on the floor and tells the children they are having a picnic. She says it saves her having to vacuum or clean up under tables.

Tip: If people are going to sit on the floor, it might be a good idea to put a blanket down. Especially if you have gum chewers in your family!

When and how you have people to your home will depend on your personality, finances, health, the time you have, and where you live.

For example, those who live in small apartments might not be able to have as many people over as those who live in a large house. They might want to suggest picnics.

When I asked women why they didn't have guests, more often than not they answered, "I can cook or clean for company, but I don't have the time or energy to do both."

My friend LuAnn says, "I used to spend hours cleaning for guests. If someone spilled something or made a mess, I would get upset. I would spend hours the day after cleaning and feeling sorry for myself. Having company was a burden, a lesson in endurance. I stopped having people over. Now all I do is put out clean towels and make sure there is extra toilet paper in the bathrooms, pick up any loose papers or clothes lying around, prepare some food, and ask people over. It is a lot less stressful. Now I actually enjoy having people to my home."

Barbara, another friend, says, "It doesn't bother me if someone spills something, but it does bother me to have guests when I haven't cleaned. I work long hours and can't cook and clean, so I don't have company."

What can Barbara do if she wants to have company but wants to feel comfortable doing it? She can call friends and say, "I'm having a potluck after church. Would you like to come? I'll do the cleaning and supply the drink and bread. How would you like to supply the entree and salad."

One of my friends, Chris, says that she and her family don't like large church potlucks, but she doesn't mind taking a dish or two to someone else's home.

Gail, another friend, says her family loves church potlucks because the children can be with their friends and the adults can visit. "Quite often," she says, "this is how we first get to know someone. I may then feel comfortable inviting them to our home."

Each person likes to do something different. We all need to do what makes us feel comfortable and what we can with our health and finances. Do the type of hospitality that works for you, even if it means having someone sit on the floor.

Prayer:
Lord, please help me to have a home
where my family and friends feel welcome and loved.

CHAPTER EIGHT

Alternative Hospitality

E ven if you can't invite people to your home, there are still many ways to be hospitable. Being hospitable simply means being friendly, sociable, welcoming, and warmhearted.

Times do change, and so do our situations. My friend Laura, who in past years has been a gracious hostess to many, many people, now has an invalid in her home. She says she cannot cope with this person and have guests too. She does, however, take plants or flowers to those in the hospital.

A unique way of being hospitable is to give a survival basket or a day brightener.

Survival baskets

Survival baskets can be given to those who are going through a stressful time (death of family member, divorce, illness). This basket can be given in place of flowers and sometimes is nicer to give a couple of weeks after the person has had a chance to start his or her grieving.

The purpose of this survival basket is to say "I care," not "I've spent a fortune." Decide on the amount you have to spend before you start. If you want to make a bigger basket than you can afford, you may be able to get one or two others to share the costs with you. Use what you have.

If you do not have a basket, you can use:

- A gift bag
- A plain bag on which you've glued pictures or bonded fabric
- A gallon jar—you can put ribbon around the lid or cut a circle of fabric one and a half inches larger than the lid of the jar; lay the fabric over the top and secure around the neck of the jar with a rubber band or tie a bow around the jar or jar lid.
- Decorative tin such as a cookie or candy tin
- Shoe box or bottom of any box that can be covered with fabric, gift wrap, contact paper, or wallpaper. You can get used wallpaper books or buy one roll of wallpaper on sale that will last for a long time.

If you wait until you can get everything perfect, you will probably not get a basket made.

What you place in the basket will depend on what you already have, what you want to spend, and how well you know the recipient.

When I'm making a survival basket, I send a quick request to God: "Lord, You know I have only five dollars to spend today. Please help me find what will be helpful to_____."

Place a note or card in the basket stating something like "just wanted to let you know that though I can't ease the pain, I care."

Hint: Individual items can be left as is, wrapped in plastic wrap, or put into a plastic bag.

The secret to the survival basket is to attach a note to some of the things. Use glue, paper tied to a ribbon, or peel-and-stick labels that have been decorated with a rubber stamp (leave plain or color with colored pencils). The note will explain to the recipient how that particular article can be used:

- Kleenex (box or pocket/purse size)—for tears
- Herbal teas, hot chocolate, or apple cider—for sharing with a friend when you need to talk with someone. (You can use a box or individual packages that have been placed in groups of four and wrapped with plastic wrap or placed in a plastic bag and tied with a bow.)
- Note cards—to write a letter of encouragement to a friend
- Stamps or book of stamps—to send those notes
- Mailing labels—to save you time. You can make labels with the computer, or if you have time, you can order a rubber stamp.
- Nerf ball—to throw when you get angry
- Empty journal—to write down your thoughts
- Bath salts or herbs—for a relaxing bath

◎ Stuffed animal—to cuddle when you get lonely
◎ Other things that could go in a basket: a bookmark, a book, a refrigerator magnet, something to munch on.

You might want to have a basic "recipe" for a survival basket that includes items based on how much you feel you can spend at the time. Here are some suggestions:

Under five dollars: pocket-size Kleenex, four packets of hot drink, four note cards, four stamps, bookmark, four mailing labels, a couple of individually wrapped pieces of candy, one packet of bath salts or a small bottle of herbal drops to put into bath.

Under ten dollars: same as above but add a journal or a small book.

Under fifteen dollars: add a stuffed animal or a book.

Hint when giving books: some people like to write lovely messages inside the book they are giving. I like to write the message on a card. If the recipient wants to copy it into the book or wants me to, that's fine. However, because I'm at the decluttering stage of my life, I like to leave the inside of the book blank. After reading it, the recipient can either give it away or take it to a used bookstore if he or she so desires. (Not this book, of course.) You might like to write in a book, such as a child's book, that might be handed down from generation to generation.

Day brighteners

My friend Dorothy gives day brighteners. She explains that day brighteners are little gifts to warm people's hearts.

Her suggestions for day brighteners include a package of pretty napkins or dish towels.

To wrap her package, Dorothy says she buys bows on sale or uses alternatives to bows. Once for a baby gift she stuck a rattle into a pair of girls' socks. She had slipped one sock inside the other and fluffed it so it looked a bit like a flower.

If I tried doing something like that, I won't tell you what it would look like, but it definitely wouldn't look like a flower. Which leads me to write: *Never compare the way you do something with the way someone else might do it!*

Some people are very creative and can make beautifully decorated packages. Others can only make the kind of bow we learned when we learned to tie our shoes. I took a one-hour class on how to make a bow and came home with flat ribbon. Then I took a two-hour class on how to make a bow and came home with flat ribbon. Finally, my son said, "Mom, just buy the bow!" Baskets or gifts do not need bows. The main idea is to give the gift. While we want it to look pretty, we do not want to spend a lot of time or money to make it. If we spend too much of our time or money, we will not want to give another one. Remember, these are simple gifts to say I care.

Budget-saving hints for making survival baskets or day brighteners:

⊚ Buy large boxes of individually packaged herbal tea bags, apple cider, or hot chocolate. You can place four

to six packages in plastic wrap or a plastic bag and tie
with a bow.

◉ Buy large packages of pocket/purse size Kleenex.

◉ Buy packages or boxes of eight or twelve note cards and
separate them into groups of four. You can wrap a
ribbon around them or place them in plastic wrap or a
Baggie.

◉ Look on the reduced tables in bookstores, drug stores,
or department stores.

◉ Buy journals in packages of two or three.

◉ Buy large packages of dish towels and napkins. You
then can split them into smaller packages.

◉ Buy tissue paper and/or wrapping paper on sale. You
can use white and stamp or color it if you wish. After
Christmas is a good time to buy white paper.

◉ If you do not have tissue paper, you can use cotton
swabs, a pretty napkin, a piece of fabric, a doily, or
other paper.

◉ Buy fabric ribbon on sale in fabric stores. It is often
cheaper to buy and easier to use than the slippery
gift-wrap ribbon.

Use your hobby. If you like baking, cookies, brownies,
or a loaf of bread can be a great day brightener. If sewing is
your hobby, make a potholder or other small gift. Others
may want to make note cards, refrigerator magnets, or
other small items. If you enjoy gardening; plants, cut flowers, a jar of jam, or fresh or canned fruit or vegetables can
say "I care."

Some other ways we can be hospitable:

- Write thank-you notes to someone who has taken part in a program or who faithfully does a certain job.
- Write encouragement notes to someone who is ill.
- An "I prayed for you today" note to almost anyone.
- Make phone calls to the elderly or shut-in.
- Meet a group at a designated spot to go walking, bicycle riding, or hiking.
- Choose a place that a group can meet for a picnic anytime. When I was young, there was a certain spot in a park where families would meet. This was not always planned as a group, but whoever wanted to would be there. Lots of times if a family didn't come for lunch, they would come after lunch and visit.
- Take someone to church, a program, or a sports event.
- Baby-sit for someone who needs a break such as a parent or a caretaker of an ill person or an elderly person.
- Take or mail the church bulletin or a tape of a sermon to someone who can't attend the church service.
- Run errands for someone who can't get out or call and say, "I'm going to such and such a store or the post office. Do you need anything?"
- Take someone shopping, to the dentist's or the physician's office, to the post office, or to the library.
- Pick up a form so a shut-in can order stamps by mail. The person may also need help in filling out the form.
- Give a half hour or hour of your time to work in

someone's garden. This can be done not only for the sick or the elderly, but for the person who is very busy or has a special day like a wedding coming up and wants everything to look nice.

- Write a letter for someone who can't or sit with someone and write checks or help to pay bills.
- Help to can fruit or vegetables.
- Read to a blind person. If time or transportation is a problem, you can read over the phone.
- In church or other meetings, sit beside a parent with children and help to keep the children occupied. You can keep something in your purse for children to play with or bring along a surprise bag.
- Share your garden produce.
- If the weather is exceptionally hot or cold, check on the elderly, the ill, or the person living alone.
- Cut grass or shovel snow.
- Give a cutting from a houseplant.
- Do laundry for someone.
- Take a half hour or an hour and help clean house for a person who is unable to clean her own home or who is planning a special event at her place.
- Invite another family or two or three to go camping.
- After reading an inspirational book that has been a blessing to you, write your name in it, pass it to someone else, and tell her to add her name. As each person reads the book, she prays for the people with their names already written in the book.
- If you are busy but have money and want to do some-

thing, find someone who may have the time but not the money and offer to supply or pay for whatever needs to be done.

Use your talents or hobbies:

- Baking—casseroles, desserts, bread or take a complete meal to a shut-in.
- Sewing—potholders or sachets for drawers.
- Crocheting—dishrags.
- Tole painting—knickknacks.
- Gardening—jar of jam, a pint of frozen berries, or a jar of fruit.
- Videotaping—tape a program for someone who can't attend and give him or her a copy.

Go together with two or three others to pay for someone to:

- Have a professional massage
- Go to a program
- Have a weekend away
- Go to a restaurant
- Attend a seminar
- Go to a retreat
- Have their house professionally cleaned

You can even do things anonymously if you prefer, although it is often nice to know who has done the kindness.

Remember, don't try to do too many things. Pick one thing that fits with your personality and with your energy, time, and money situation. Jesus loves you even if at this time all you can do is smile!

Prayer:
Dear Lord, please help me to find something
within my abilities and finances
to help _____ today.

CHAPTER NINE

Not for Women Only

en are hospitable too. In preparation for writing this chapter, I interviewed several men and got their ideas.

Most things throughout this book can be done by either a man or a woman. And most things in this chapter can be done by a woman. However, I am writing this chapter because of a special request. More and more women are working outside the home, and more and more husbands are helping with housework, meals, and hospitality. Many single men also make good hosts (women, don't call asking where to find one!).

The best thing a man can do to help his wife is to know the overall plan. This might mean that the best thing he can do is to stay clear of the cook (or to keep guests clear of the cook) and the kitchen.

A retired pastor stated, "If a husband wants guests, then maybe it is his responsibility to help make it possible by doing whatever may be necessary, rather than expecting his wife to do all the preparation. This could include vacuuming, picking up around the house, or making an entree. Before the meal and after the meal, the husband should do more than entertain the visitors. He can do things such as setting up chairs and helping with the children.

"The wife is usually the person under pressure in a hospitality situation. After church I like to suggest we ask someone to bring what they have and join us in the park. This is easier than planning for guests for a week or two ahead, which places pressure on the wife. Hospitality should be a family affair. Children should be encouraged to do different things. Sometimes they can do the dishes, but this should not always be their job. They can make the punch or cookies. Be sure to mention what they have contributed to the meal!"

I have a friend who is unable to help with any cooking or cleaning up. When she and her husband go to someone else's home, her husband volunteers to help. He does a great job!

Some ways a man can help his wife:

⊚ Cook
⊚ Clean the bathroom
⊚ Vacuum
⊚ Dust
⊚ Scrub the kitchen floor

- Buy the groceries
- Put food away
- Do the dishes (one man said that when he knows he is going to do dishes, he makes sure paper plates are used).

If a single man cannot cook, he can:

- Buy prepared foods
- Have two or three friends join together to put on a large meal
- Take people to a restaurant

If a man is going to a potluck and doesn't want to cook, he can take:

- Juice
- Bread
- Prepared dessert
- A fresh vegetable tray

Other hospitality ideas men suggested they could do:

- Take a shut-in for a drive
- Greet people at church, letting them know they were missed if they have been gone
- Clean gutters on someone's house
- Help to fix things inside a house
- Teach someone to use a computer

◉ Take an elderly or handicapped person to church or
   someplace fun
◉ Use professional skills to help someone

No matter what type of hospitality men choose, Jesus
loves them too.

Prayer:
Lord, please help men
to feel comfortable being hospitable.

CHAPTER TEN

You Don't Need a Guest Room

It is not necessary to have a separate guest room in order to have guests stay overnight. When giving the invitation to possible guests, tell them what you have. "We have a separate room." "Our living-room couch makes into a bed." "If you can bring sleeping bags and are willing to sleep on the floor, we have a place for you." If they need accommodations beyond what you can offer, they will look elsewhere.

Potential guests also appreciate knowing what you have planned. "I'll be working, so you will be on your own for entertainment and meals." "I'll be able to take a few days off. What would you enjoy doing?" Everyone is more comfortable when they know what to expect.

Recently, the singles had a retreat near us. My friend

Melissa told me she had wall-to-wall sleeping bags in almost every room of her house. She said she told her guests before they came and again when they arrived, "I ask only three things of you when you stay with me. First, I do not have the time or energy to cook for you; however, you are welcome to use the kitchen. Second, after you bathe or shower, please use the towel to wipe the tub or shower, then place the towel in the dirty laundry. Third, please do not use my laundry facilities."

Once, when we had company, I had planned to give up our bed for our guests. The wife said, "Don't ever give up your bed for guests. The host and hostess must be able to function at peak efficiency when they have guests." That was over twenty years ago, and through the years I have come to appreciate her good advice.

What about children giving up their beds? Sometimes it can be fun for all the children to sleep in a tent or in the living room. Let someone else use their bed but only after you have asked your children's permission. Sometimes guests like to look through cupboards or drawers. If you know your guests may be like that, don't let them use your children's rooms. Your children should be allowed their privacy too.

If you have animals, be sure to state, "I have a pet (dog, cat, skunk, boa constrictor) and hope that won't be a problem."

A good friend or family member may be coming to your area whether for just one night or several. It may not be a good time for you (emotionally, financially, or physically).

Tell them. Don't feel guilty. Say, "Now is not a good time for us to have company." Don't let them or anyone else persuade you otherwise. You may offer to make a reservation somewhere for them. Let them know that you will contact them about the cost, or if you want to pay for their reservations, tell them.

When someone you love is coming to the area and you issue an invitation and they decline, don't take it personally. They may have a special need to make other arrangements.

To the overnight guest

Don't assume that because the people are friends or family members, they will automatically be able to accommodate you. If you will be coming and going at all hours, it might be better to find somewhere else to stay.

If you are allergic to animals and your host or hostess has animals, don't expect them to throw their pet out. You may have to plan on staying elsewhere. If they offer to pay for a motel, don't be offended. On the other hand, don't *expect* them to pay.

When your intended host or hostess says it is not a good time, don't take it personally. Respect his or her right to say No.

When someone in your home has been ill or you are sick, do not plan to stay with anyone. If you must travel, stay in a motel. Even if the people insist. Peggy, a friend, said that she insisted someone stay with her. Some of the guests had been vomiting and were vomiting in her home. She said she and her husband both got sick and were flat in bed for two days. It took them three weeks to feel better. She said, "Never again will I issue an invitation to someone who is ill. Especially if they have the money to stay in a hotel. Regardless of the circumstances."

If someone will be picking you up at an airport, bus, boat, or train station, try to plan your arrival time so that person won't have to travel in rush-hour traffic or at any inconvenient time.

When you leave, offer to take the sheets off the bed and remake the bed with clean sheets. Respect the wishes of your host or hostess.

Anytime my family was traveling, my dad always said, "After three days, people (friends or family) and fish stink." Don't wear out your welcome.

Prayer:
Lord, please help us to welcome overnight guests
when we are able. But also give us the courage
to say No when it is not a good time for us.

CHAPTER ELEVEN

Fill 'er Up!

A car needs gas in its tank to go. A Christian hostess needs to have her spiritual tank filled by the Lord before she can give to others. She cannot be an effective witness if she's trying to run on empty.

How a person's spiritual tank is filled will differ from person to person. Spending some time each morning in prayer and study can give us a sense of peace for the day. We all have different situations. Some people say you should spend an hour first thing every morning in private worship.

If you can do this, great. This may, however, be impractical for the young working mother. Besides taking her own shower, she may need to prepare breakfast, get the children up, drop the children at the day care, and be at her job at 7:00 a.m. This means she probably will be unable to spend one whole hour first thing.

Some people get up one hour earlier. If a person is already getting to bed at 11:00 p.m. or midnight and getting up at 5:30 a.m., one hour early is not practical. It is discouraging to that person to have someone say, "Oh, just get up an hour earlier."

If a person tries to do something that doesn't fit into her schedule, she might get discouraged. She may say, "I can't do it."

Some people have to eat first thing in the morning. Each of us needs to find what works best for us.

Here are some suggestions for different ways to find time for God:

- Spend the first hour after getting up in private worship.
- Spend fifteen minutes after waking up in worship and then have certain times of the day to pray for certain people or projects.
- The busy stay-at-home woman might take an hour or part of an hour after she has her husband and all the children out the door.
- Another woman might be better spending her hour just before everyone comes home in the afternoon.
- Spend an hour each evening. (Some people are night owls who won't fall asleep like the rest of us might do.)

Here are some suggestions of ways to improve your time with God:

◉ Have a prayer partner—you can pray over the phone if not physically together. It is good to have a set time to pray together and let nothing interfere with the time for your prayer partnership. However, having a special person to pray with at any time is also a help.

◉ Attend a religious seminar.

◉ Attend a weekend retreat. (My husband usually makes sure I go at least once a year.) When our son was at home, it was their special weekend to plan and do things together. It is the one weekend a year my husband doesn't hear "Honey do." He figures the peace is worth the cost. Seriously, he says he can tell I come home invigorated by being with the women, hearing inspirational speakers, and attending prayer groups.

◉ Attend a Bible class during the week.

◉ Attend church services.

◉ Watch a religious program on video.

◉ Listen to a religious CD or cassette.

◉ Read an inspiring book.

◉ Listen to or sing or play religious music.

◉ Write a note to someone telling them you have especially prayed for them on that day. My friends really appreciate it when I do this.

◉ Collect and share quotes on prayer or other spiritual subjects.

◉ Keep a journal. There are many different ways of keeping a journal. Here are some suggestions:

1. Use a notebook. Write prayer requests in the front and answers to prayer in the back.

2. Use a notebook and record prayer requests on the top half of the page, answers on the bottom half.

3. Use a notebook and use one page for requests and the page across from it for answers.

4. Use a very detailed journal with tabs that divide the book or loose-leaf binder into sections to write different things in.

5. Use a notebook and write in your thoughts on Bible texts.

6. Use your computer to write notes.

There are many different types of journals at Christian bookstores. Whether you buy or make a prayer journal might depend on your finances.

When I first started to journal, I tried to use a journal that was very detailed. It had about sixteen divisions in it. I used it for about a week and never used each division, so I gave up and decided to create my own journal, using a loose-leaf binder and 5- by 8- inch paper.

I like some detail, but not too much, so I made four dividers with tabs. Each tab represented a letter in the word **PRAY** (I'll explain the significance of each letter in a moment). I do not have each section divided into days or weeks. This allows me to write as much as I want in each section. Some days one section might have more than another. Each day I just write down the date. This makes it fun to look back and see when I made a certain request and when it might have been answered.

P stands for praise. In this section I write what I am especially thankful for and also answers to prayer. Some days, if the day before has been a day I would rather forget, all I may write is "Thank You for Jesus." (I know that it is good to give thanks and praise, and it can raise your spirits for the day. I also think it is good to be honest and say "Lord, all I really feel like thanking You today for is _____," or just simply "Thank You for Jesus." The Lord loves us no matter how we feel.

R is for read. Here I read a verse or two from the Bible. Some days I might pick one verse. Other days I might choose to read four or ten. It will depend on what the verse is saying. I then put in my own words what the verse or verses are saying to me. For instance, in the book of John, I might read the verse: "When Jesus heard that, he said, 'This sickness is not unto death, but for the glory of God, that the Son of God might be glorified thereby' " (John 11:4).

If I am really feeling ill and don't know if I'm going to die, I might write: "OK, Lord, I know that regardless of how sick I get or how ill I'm feeling, even if it takes my physical life, it can't take away the fact that You died on the cross so I could have a home in heaven. If I am going to die, help how I handle it and let my belief in Your love be a witness for You.

If I am feeling OK, I might write, "Lord, as long as You give me life, I will try to make this diseased old body a witness for You," or I could write, "Lord, are You trying to tell me that instead of feeling sorry for myself today, I need to be helping someone else to cope with something in her life? If so, Lord, put that person in my path. Give me the love, compassion, and wisdom that I will need to pass a blessing on to her."

The books of Psalms, Proverbs, and John have been especially helpful to me.

A stands for ask. It is here that I write out my requests for the day. It is fun to look back and see when the first request was made and when it was answered. The answers aren't always Yes. Sometimes there is no direct answer, but there are enough answers to tell me I do have a God who cares and is in control.

Y is for yield. All I write here is: in Your way, in Your time, or Your will. It reminds me that the Lord is in charge. Sometimes when I write *in Your time*, I feel like adding *but hurry up about it*. Over and over I have had to learn that the Lord's timing is best.

I like using the word PRAY because it is so simple and easy to remember that it can be taught to a child. It also makes it easy to go through each step whether I want to take fifteen minutes or an hour for my devotions.

Remember, if you choose to journal, there is no right or wrong way to journal. Do whatever works out best for you.

Under no circumstances should you read someone else's prayer journal. I was taught never to read someone else's letters, diaries, or journals. However, I have friends who, when they visit me, I have to hide everything. One even brags about having read someone's journal when that person lived with them. She even tells what that poor individual wrote. This may be the reason a wife, husband, or child doesn't journal. She or he might think (or know) that someone else will read it.

What hinders you or helps you in having your private devotions?

The main thing is to have private time praying and studying. Always keep some spiritual fuel in your tank.

Prayer:
Lord, please help me to make time
for You each day.

CHAPTER TWELVE

Healthy Hospitality

$\mathscr{B}$e hospitable to yourself. Make your health second only to God in your life. Many women are so busy they don't think about their own health. If it is not made a priority, in twenty years you may have poor health and find it harder to be hospitable. If you are healthy, you can interact better with others.

Health includes emotional and mental attitude as well as physical strength. To keep healthy, you need to be mentally and physically active and take time for rest and relaxation. It depends where you are in your life, what you will need to do to keep healthy.

A few weeks ago, my husband and I were walking down the street. Three little boys racing and weaving their bicycles whizzed by. My husband asked in a shocked voice,

"Did you hear what that boy said?"

"No," I answered.

He said, "Watch out for those old people!"

I burst out laughing. My husband didn't think it was funny. He likes to think he's twenty-nine and holding. For days afterward when he would think about it, he would mumble and groan. When I would think about it, I would laugh. Some days I feel nine. Some days I feel ninety. I try to enjoy life no matter how old someone else may think I am.

To the two of us "old people," sixty is looking younger and younger. We think old age might be when you reach ninety. Your attitude can help you no matter how old you are. However, if we make our health a priority, "old age" can be a lot easier. We will be able to enjoy being older if our health is good.

Each woman may have to do something different to remain healthy. The person with a mentally stressful job will need to do physical activity and do whatever it takes to relax. A person who is physically active all day will need relaxation and mental stimulation. The woman who is constantly eating on the run will need to change her eating habits. Whatever your need is, I hope you find something useful in my lists of ways to improve physical, mental, and emotional health (we dealt with spiritual health in chapter 11).

Suggestions for physical exercise:

Outside: walking, swimming, running, bicycling (can be done as a family).

Inside: stand in front of the TV and march in place. Get everyone off the couch and get moving! Lift weights—you can start out with six-ounce cans and work up to larger sizes.

If you can afford an exercise machine but don't have room, put it in the living room or dining room.(You'll be more apt to use it if you can see it.)

Exercise during your coffee break or lunch hour at work. Walk stairs.

Physically handicapped: get someone else to move your muscles for you. I know someone who rides a stationary bike for five minutes, then rests. There are exercise videos available even for people in wheelchairs.

You may notice I didn't include carrying your purse as a physical activity. There is no doubt that it is a very physical activity. Some of our purses are so big and full they could hide a gravel truck. Carrying such a load is not good exercise. It can be dangerous to shoulder and arm muscles. If you have a big purse, then maybe for your health you need to get a smaller purse. If you have an overwhelming need or desire to carry a lot of "stuff," put a bag or briefcase into the car and select items to carry with you only when you absolutely need them.

Suggestions for mental stimulation:
- Borrow and read a book from the library.
- Take a class. (You can do this with videos you get from a library or school.)

Suggestions for relaxation:

- Work on a hobby. What is a relaxing hobby for one person might not be for another. I have a friend who is a beautiful seamstress, and sewing relaxes her. If I tried it, I'd be so full of tension I'd need to visit a spa. To some people, working in the garden is relaxing; to others it is a chore.
- Pick a family hobby such as collecting shells, making something, or bird watching.
- Borrow a funny book, video, cassette tape, or compact disc from the library.
- Soak in a nice warm tub.
- Pay to have a professional massage. This can be a nice gift to give yourself.

Suggestions for improving your eating habits:

- Eat simpler meals.
- Eat plain foods that don't take hours to cook.
- Make sure the family eats one meal together every day.
- If you are living alone, you may want to plan on eating with someone else at least a couple of times a week.
- If eating too much is a problem, eat only when you sit down to the table. Don't allow eating in any room other than the kitchen or dining room.

Everyone must decide what to do to stay healthy. It doesn't matter what you choose. Just say to yourself: "I will choose to do something for my health today. I will take fifteen minutes and make my health a priority."

Whatever you choose to do for your health, you may like to do it with someone else. This is especially true of exercising. I have some friends who walk together every morning at 8:30. If you have a specific time and place and someone to exercise with, you will have encouragement to continue. You might enjoy taking a class or joining a club with people who like to do the same things.

If we would make health a priority for ourselves and include our families in some of our activities, then maybe we would encourage the other members of our families to make their health a priority.

Don't feel guilty if your home is not clean or if you cannot have company. If at this time for your emotional, mental, or physical health you cannot even have a close friend or family member to your home, don't. Just say, "I am unable at this time to accommodate you," if someone asks to come.

If you have to choose fifteen minutes for your health or fifteen minutes for cleaning your house, choose your health. If you have to choose fifteen minutes for your health or fifteen minutes for being hospitable, choose your health. Jesus loves you and knows you'll be happiest if you're healthy.

Prayer:
Lord, please help me make health a priority
only after You. Help me put my health
before cleaning or hospitality.

CHAPTER THIRTEEN

$\mathscr{T}$he problems in our lives are like onions. Onions can cause tears. Problems can cause tears. Onions smell stronger as each layer is peeled away. As we work through our problems, each step may hurt. But remember that when an onion has been peeled and added to a recipe, it flavors the food. After you have dealt with a problem, you may feel better, and it may help you empathize with others dealing with a similar problem.

If we don't learn how to deal with our problems, we might be unable to be hospitable.

Everyone has an onion or two or three or four in her life. Christ had to deal with stressful situations. He had onions in His life.

Some onions are large and some are small. What might

seem like a large onion to some will seem like a small onion to others. While you are dealing with a problem, it might seem large, but afterward you may look back and see that it was small.

This happened to me last summer. I thought I had encountered a series of large onions when I was trying to learn a different software program. I am convinced that the people who write software programs speak and write in a different language than I do. They must also think out of a different side of the brain.

Usually, when I would run into problems, I would call my son. He would ask, "Now what did you do?"

I would answer, "If I knew, I wouldn't be calling."

He would say, "What does the screen look like?"

I would tell him, then he would patiently walk me through the problem.

One day he was not available when I had a major problem. My husband saw my frustration and my tears. He listened to the not too nice words I uttered. He suggested I call the software publisher. I did. A courteous gentleman answered the phone. He asked, "May I help you?"

"You certainly can!" I said. "The first thing I want to know is whether the president of the company (I used his name) pays for wigs for those of us who pull out all our hair trying to use his programs!"

Silence. Then the man responded, "Well, lady, you are my last customer for the day. If I can help you, it will make my day."

The first thing he said to do was, "Look at the toolbar."

I asked, "Toolbar? What is a toolbar?"

He answered, "See those lines at the top of the screen with the pictures? They are called toolbars."

I would never have guessed. None of those pictures look like tools to me.

I wanted to put dots beside one of the lines that I had written. Those little dots are called bullets. Here the term fit. I would try to put a dot beside one line. Dots would appear beside every line on the page. I would try to erase the extra dots. Whiz, all the dots would disappear. So would every line on the page. The kind gentleman was a big help. I finally learned.

However, he did not tell me I had made his day. As he hung up, he probably said, "Thank You, Lord, that she was my last customer for today. I could not take another one like her!"

I wonder if he thought I was an onion in his life?

I think my husband purposely schedules his life so he'll either be at work or asleep when I turn on the computer. When he does help me, the language we use is not the language we learned at Marriage Encounter.

One day we had a friend's boy staying with us. He said, "Bev, you shouldn't yell at Don."

I said, "I'm not yelling at Don, I'm yelling at the computer!"

Our printer died just as I needed to print some pages. A friend kindly loaned us hers. The first time I needed to print out a page, all I did was click the arrow on the printer picture. Lo and behold, a page came out of the printer! I was so proud of myself.

In about an hour, I needed to print ten consecutive pages. I clicked on the printer picture. Nothing happened. I clicked on the picture again. Nothing. When nothing happened the third time, I figured the key must be stuck. So I quickly clicked on the picture twelve more times. All of a sudden, the printer started to print. It wouldn't stop. Forty pages later, I figured I should do something. I looked for an off button on the printer. I couldn't see one. Quickly, I ran into the bedroom and woke up my husband.

"Come quick, come quick. I'm sorry to bother you, but this is a national emergency. If you don't stop the printer, all three thousand sheets will be printed on!"

My husband calmly walked out reached around and under the printer and turned it off. I figure if they mean for you to turn off a printer, they should put the off button up where you can see it!

Those were little onions in my life.

It's easy to try to ignore onions, but it's usually better to deal with them sooner instead of putting it off to the last minute.

If only I had taken that advice when I needed to get a driver's license. We were living in a small town with only one examiner. The woman who did my hair said, "Don't worry about it. My husband is the examiner, and he always passes the young women."

I used every delaying device known, but one day my husband, who was working for the forest service, came home and said, "We have been called out to fight a fire. We may be gone several days. You can't be stranded here with a baby. It is too far for you to walk to town. You must get your license."

So I went to get my license.

The first thing the examiner did was to stand in front of the car and ask me to turn on the signals. He waited. Then he repeated, "Turn on your signals."

I said, "They are on."

He said, "Is the key turned on?"

I said No and promptly turned on the key and stepped on the gas. You should have seen him jump for the sidewalk!

Then he went around to the back of the car. This time he stayed on the sidewalk. Again he said, "Turn on your signals. Again he waited. Then he repeated, "Turn on your signals."

"They are on!" I said.

"Is the key on?" he asked. . . .

As he got in beside me, he probably sent up a quick prayer for extra protection.

He instructed me to pull away from the curb, turn at the first corner, and drive up a hill. "Park here," he said halfway up the hill.

I stopped the car. He waited for a minute or two. He looked at me and asked, "Are you parked?"

"Yes," I answered. I was afraid to do anything else but stop. It was a steep hill. The car could have rolled backward. As we pulled away, I realized I had been about four feet from the curb.

"OK, drive around the next block. When you get to the alley, stop," he said.

I drove around the block and stopped.

"Now back into that alley," he said.

I missed a large pole on the corner by about two or three inches.

"OK, pull out and drive down this road three blocks."

I was doing just great until a logging truck came toward me. I started to slow down. The inspector said, "You are OK; just keep going."

I thought to myself, "It's OK for you to say, buddy. Those big logs aren't on your side."

He picked a street with no parked cars and had me parallel park. I wondered why but wasn't going to ask any questions. I probably took a little extra space but managed to park quite well. It was the only time in my life I managed to parallel park.

"Drive back to the office," he said.

Before we got out of the car, he asked me to do hand signals. By this time, I was so rattled I couldn't even remember if I had hands. The only good thing was that my left hand was closest to the window, so I'm sure I used the proper hand. I don't know if I did the signals right. All I wanted to do was go home and have a good cry.

"Come in and get your license," he said.

"Get my license!" I squeaked. Then I realized the poor man didn't want to risk life and limb to give me another exam.

When we got up to the counter he said, "That will be seven dollars."

I reached into my purse and gave him all the one dollar bills I had. "I am sorry, I will have to go home and get the rest of the money," I said.

With a disgusted voice, he said, "Lady, you already gave me the seven dollars."

So I got my license. It was a large onion in my life. I am sure it was a large onion in his life too. It might not have seemed so large if I had handled it earlier, when I wasn't under so much pressure.

Is there anyone who doesn't have onions in her life? About four years ago at a women's retreat, I ended up in the same prayer group as a woman who I thought had it all together. Every time I saw her, even on a hot summer day, every strand of hair was in place, her makeup complemented her coloring, and she didn't have one wrinkle in her dress. She always looked like a lady. I sometimes look like something the dog dragged in. Especially on a hot summer day! She gives seminars on organization, while I give seminars on survival. She gives tours of her home and opens up her closets to show how you can be organized. If I showed you some of my closets, you would need to have your life insurance up to date, put on a hard hat, and stand back while I opened the doors. How on earth was I going to relate to this woman?

We got to know each other. We prayed for each other's needs. And I learned that she had problems too. They were just different than my problems. I don't remember the specific things we prayed about. When we see each other now, I am happy to greet her. In the past, I would have gone down a different aisle in the supermarket to avoid her.

When dealing with a problem in your life, you may hear, read, or see something an expert says to do. Remember that it is only a suggestion. If it works for you, great. If not, look elsewhere for help.

As Christians, we know that our heavenly Father can be the biggest source of our help. I would like you to remember two words when faced with a problem: *Carry On*.

Christ is   **O**nward
Always   **N**ow
Ready to
Rescue
You

The **CARRY** is Christ's part. The **Onward Now** is our part. In this chapter I am hoping you will find something that might help you go onward. Something to help you work through your problems.

Your finances will help to determine how you can deal with problems. If you are on a tight budget, you might need to find free sources of help and information. My list of places to look for help includes:

- Support groups
- Books, magazines, newsletters
- Cassette tapes (check your church or public library)
- Videos

⊚ Lectures and seminars
⊚ Professional advice

Personalities differ. I was a premature baby and have been trying to run ahead of the Lord ever since. You know the type. One of the ones who prays, Come on, Lord, come on, as we run down the street. Another woman prays and expects the Lord to drop something from heaven. Sometimes He does. But because he doesn't always answer this way, this woman may never make a decision. Still, a third woman will methodically gather information, then pray about it and make a decision. A fourth woman will have to be poked with a cattle prod just to think about the problem, never mind pray about it.

Some of us have personalities that are so high-strung we could be trapeze artists. Others of us are so laid back that a train could run over us and we wouldn't notice it.

We need to know that we can deal with a problem more effectively if we deal with it according to our personality and not someone else's.

Each person will be working with different time constraints. When considering how to handle a problem, we need to take into consideration the time frame we have and need.

When we have onions in our lives, we need to learn how to cope if we are to remain emotionally healthy. I can spend all my time thinking *poor me*. I can blame someone else for my problems, or I can choose to go on with my life. What will it be?

Onions may, and usually do, bring tears. It is OK to cry. Just because we have learned how to cope with a problem doesn't mean we won't still have days when we will cry or feel depressed. One sure way to become depressed in learning how to cope is by comparing yourself to someone else.

A number of years ago, we lived on my brother's farm. I would go out in the morning for about an hour and help my brother and sister-in-law feed the sheep and work in the tomatoes. I would be exhausted for the rest of the day. My sister-in-law would go in, clean, cook, and bake. Would that depress me!

But rather than getting depressed, why not find out what we can learn from the person who can do something we can't? I still vividly recall the day I slithered into class in college, hoping no one had noticed me. I was sitting waiting for class to start when in walked another female student. Her hair and makeup were done to perfection. Guess who she sat by.

Before class started I learned that this woman was the nursing supervisor of one nursing unit and acting supervisor of another nursing unit at the local hospital. She was taking classes for her master's degree. As I got to know her better, I learned that she was helping her husband with lectures four nights a week, she walked two miles before work every day, and had company for dinner every week after church.

After I got past the point of wanting to kick her for proving some people are near perfection, I thought I'd better learn from this lady quick. I asked her how she did everything. She said the secret was simplification. She never made fancy dishes. In fact, she served plain rice or potatoes and put different toppings out. She kept everything simple at home.

In learning how to cope, we need to first state what the problem is. Then learn as much as we can about the problem.

When Lazarus died, how did Jesus handle the situation? Did He say to Mary and Martha, "Just pray about it, and Lazarus will walk right through that door"? No. First, He wept. He showed emotion and compassion. Then He said, "Roll away the stone." Then He prayed. Then He said, "Unwrap him" (see John 11:32-44).

Jesus was showing us how to cope. First, showing emotions is OK. Second, admit what the problem is. Third, pray about it. Fourth, learn how to deal with it.

How did Jesus handle an onion in His life? When He hung on the cross, His mother stood nearby sobbing.

Jesus said to His mother, "Mother, here is someone to act as your son." Did He say to her:

- Mother, don't be so emotional. Quit your crying.
- Mom, just pray about it, and everything will be all right.
- Mom, God has let this happen for a reason, and you'll understand it someday.
- Mother, this might be the only way that you can have a home in heaven.

No. What He did say conveyed the message:

◉ I care about you.
◉ I cannot look after you myself, but I have found someone who can.
◉ At this time in your life, you need someone with skin on to give you a hug.

Might Jesus be saying to us:

◉ You may not be able to care for someone, but you may be able to find someone who can.
◉ When you are dealing with an onion in your life, you probably will need someone with skin on to be there for you.
◉ Maybe sometime you might be the "skin on" for someone else.

Have you ever said or had someone say to you, "Just pray about it"?

My friend Dawn says that nothing annoys her more than when someone says to her, Just pray about it. She adds, "What is that person trying to tell me: I haven't prayed about it; I haven't prayed hard enough; my prayers aren't reaching God; all I need is prayer? In reality, what I may need is a hug, counseling, or other practical help.

Saying "just pray about it" is different than saying, I am praying for you. Saying "just pray about it" sounds as if that's all you need. Saying, "I am praying for you" says "I am asking my heavenly Father to help you."

How we deal with a problem might not be the same way someone else will deal with it. What might seem right to someone might seem wrong to someone else. We need to deal with our problems in a way that is best for us.

However, sometimes what people think can influence a decision that we might make in dealing with a problem. A friend, Helen, told me that she had to move her own sister Sue out of one of the apartments that they owned. She said that she had to do it for both of their sakes. Helen said the hardest part was worrying what their friends would say or do.

There are two lessons here. One, not to be critical of another's choice. Two, do what we need to do for our own survival. Sometimes this may involve admitting that we're having a problem we can't handle, and turning down a request to fulfill someone else's needs.

Some people don't understand NO and may try either aggressively or through passive aggression to get you to change your mind. You need to stick to your decision.

One of my friends, Erma, was going through a hard time, and her sister and her husband were planning to stop in for a visit in two weeks. Erma called her sister and told her that she couldn't have her there at that time. Two days later the sister called with a health question. When Erma learned that the sister hadn't called her other sisters who were nurses, she realized this was just an attempt to change

Erma's mind. Two days later the sister was on the phone again, asking when she could see Erma, and reminding her that it was still two weeks until she would be coming.

Afraid she might say something she would regret later if the sister kept calling, Erma called a qualified family counselor. The counselor told her that she needed to set boundaries and stick to them. The counselor suggested she call her sister and offer to make motel arrangements for her.

The night before Erma's sister was to come through town, she and her brother-in-law called. They asked how things were going. They said they were coming through and would stay at the motel. Erma replied, "Fine. Have a good time."

Erma told me that knowing her sister, she figured she might get a phone call saying they had missed their reservations. Erma didn't want to spend all day wondering what she was going to say. Just before they were to arrive, Erma unplugged the phone and let her answering service take all the calls. Sure enough, when she plugged the phone in, about three hours later, her sister had been calling every ten minutes. Finally her sister told her they had missed their reservations, so they were staying at another motel.

Erma said she stuck to her decision even though the rest of her family didn't understand, and she was glad she did.

Husbands don't always know how we are feeling and might have to be told. Their brains tilt a different way than ours. How you approach a problem can make all the difference.

My husband says he wishes he could build a house with the furniture built in or at least nailed to the floor so I couldn't have it moved. However, a couple of months ago, we decided that even though finances were tight, we were going to have a weekly date. Once a week we planned to borrow videos from the library. The first time we watched one, I said, "Sitting in these two chairs is some date. It would be better if we could sit on the couch and cuddle." I left the room for a few minutes. When I returned, the furniture had been moved. No muttering. No complaining.

It has taken me twenty-three years, but now I know what to do to get the furniture moved. It works better than "Honey, please move the furniture."

Some people think that old age is an onion. Just recently I visited an antique mall. I didn't know whether to be impressed or depressed. Impressed at all the lovely polished antiques or depressed that lots of the dishes were my age or younger. Some days I feel like an antique. Some days I look like an unpolished one. However, as an item becomes antique, its value goes up. So I'm really more valuable than I thought I was.

Did you know that laughter is a contagious disease? If you start laughing, you may cause an epidemic.

The other day we were driving down the freeway. My husband asked, "Did you see that lady? She was all alone, but she was really laughing."

I thought, *one smart lady, using the time she had to laugh.* When you laugh, you are helping your immune system.

You are also helping yourself to cope with any situation, even if the situation isn't funny.

Have you ever done something silly, then looked around and hoped nobody was watching? Next time you do something stupid, don't bother turning around. Just say, "Lord, I hope I helped someone's immune system!"

I believe we all need to put laughter into our lives. Do you like to read books, watch videos, or listen to cassettes?

If someone asks, "Why are you reading or watching or listening to that silly thing," say, "I'm helping my immune system."

It can get you off the hook every time.

When You Have an Onion in Your Life

When there's an onion in your life,
And as it's peeling,
It sends your body, mind and senses
busy reeling.
Your heart aches,
and within your soul
you're feeling
Like you don't want to carry on.

Remember you have a God
Who does care.
State the problem.
Give it to him
to bear.

Consider your health, finances, personality, and time.
Make a decision that fits for you, and start to climb.

AND CARRY ON!

Prayer:
Heavenly Father, we know that our problems
can be like onions, causing tears and strong smells
as they are peeled away. Help us also to see
that they can add flavor to our lives.
Amen.

CHAPTER FOURTEEN

Coping, not Moping

People living with a chronic disease or handicap can still be hospitable. It seems like more and more women and men are being diagnosed with chronic diseases such as lupus, chronic fatigue, fibromyalgia, myasthenia gravis, diabetes, celiac, and multiple sclerosis that force changes in lifestyle. Learning to cope and not mope with her disability will help a woman to be a better hostess or guest.

A person who has previously been very healthy probably will face depression after being diagnosed with a chronic disease. It is natural to grieve. It is also natural to have days of depression or anger years after you have learned to cope. When this happens, it is good to look around. There is always someone else worse off. (For a friend or a relative to mention this, however, is not appropriate and may only anger the person trying to cope. Let the person discover this herself.)

Sometimes the first reaction is Why me, God? There may be a period of time when the individual doesn't want to pray or have anything to do with God or church. That is the time for the rest of her friends to just be friends and pray. Don't make her feel guilty. Give her practical help. Stand by her whether she decides to leave God out of her life or not. God doesn't give up on you. Don't expect everyone to react the way you think you would.

Some steps in learning to cope with a new disability include:

- ⊚ Gather information about the disease or disability.
- ⊚ Find a support group.
- ⊚ You may want to get more than one professional opinion.
- ⊚ Remember you are in charge.
- ⊚ Choose treatment that is best for you.
- ⊚ Help to educate your family and friends.
- ⊚ If you need financial help, work aggressively on getting it.
- ⊚ Choose to cope in a way you can, not according to how someone else does.
- ⊚ Laugh at situations when you can.
- ⊚ Decide how you can be hospitable and how you can be a good guest.

Gather information

In order to understand the disease or disability, it helps to gather information about the disease. Sometimes physicians' offices will have pamphlets about your diagnosis. The library might have information. Look for articles on the illness. There might be books about someone living with the same condition. Some organizations or medical groups have videos explaining different diseases. If you or someone you know has a computer and has access to the Internet, have them see if they can find anything about your disease. Look for phone numbers and addresses of associations or support groups. Family and friends may know of someone else with the same diagnosis who may be able to help you get information. Check with directory assistance to find out if there is a toll-free number for an association that deals with the disease.

Find a support group

When I was first diagnosed with myasthenia gravis, I felt all alone. I had never heard of the disease. One day a friend of my mother's said she thought I had the same disease as her niece. She said she thought there was a Myasthenia Gravis Association. I can't explain the relief I felt at the first meeting I attended. I met people who had had the disease for years. I heard how they coped. I learned I could overdose on the medication as well as underdose. I learned there were certain drugs I shouldn't take.

A support group may help you:

⊚ Learn more about your disease. Quite often they have guest speakers who will lead discussions on certain aspects of the disease.

- Talk to other people and see how they cope.
- Notice that there are people doing better than you but also others doing worse.
- Learn about new treatments. Your physician may not have heard about them.
- Have a support system you can call when you need extra understanding or advice.

It is important to attend support groups when first dealing with the disease. After you have dealt with it for a couple of years, you may not feel the need to attend the meetings. They are still helpful and informative, but you may not need as much support. It is good to support the association even if you don't attend all the meetings.

Getting alternate professional opinions

If after you have gathered information and attended some support groups you feel that you are receiving good medical care, great. If, however, you feel that you may want a different medical opinion, get one. You may also want to get information for alternative methods of health care.

Remember you are in charge

You are the authority on your body. After consulting with professionals and people who are living with the disease, you have the right to choose or refuse treatment.

Choose treatment that is best for you

Your physician is not a mind reader. If the treatment is not working for you or if you are having an adverse reaction, tell him or her. Quite often physicians will say that nothing you eat or do will affect your disease. This may or may not be true. Everyone reacts differently. Keep a daily log of what you eat and do and how you respond both physically and emotionally. You may find certain foods that cause problems. If certain situations stress you out, try to avoid them.

You may find something that is keeping you from feeling well. Joy, a close friend, had been diagnosed with a chronic disease. She thought that her headaches and feeling as if she was drugged and needed to sleep all the time were caused by the disease. She found out that she had a gas leak in her furnace. Once that was fixed, most of her headaches and the drugged feeling and wanting to sleep most of the time disappeared. She still has her chronic illness but is feeling much better. She could have lost her life just thinking she was having a symptom of her disease. After you have had the condition for a while, you may need to change how you take your medication. The physician can help you with this. Don't get into a life-threatening situation by trying to change something without letting your physician know.

Help to educate your family and friends

If you can take your family to your association meetings, they will be able to understand and help you more. Have written information available. You will be ready if someone says, I've never heard of that disease, or I've heard about it but don't know anything about it. This is not bragging or complaining. It does two things. One, it helps them understand. Two, it may help them pass information on to someone else who might need it.

When we go to a store or mall or attend a meeting, my husband always tries to park close to the building. If he can't find a space close, he always drops me off and then finds a place to park. I have never asked for him to do this; he is just thoughtful.

If you need financial help

One of the most discouraging things about having to change your lifestyle because of a disease is the financial situation. You may have to quit your job just when you need the extra money for drugs or treatment. If you qualify for social security or other financial assistance, apply for it. You may need to get an attorney to help you. If you do need an attorney, it is best to contact the people in the association because they may have one who has handled other cases like yours.

If you have worked and now have to go on disability, it can be hard to accept. Just apply for all the help you might be able to get.

Cope in a manner that works best for you

Each person has to cope with her disability however is best for her. Even two people with the same disease will cope differently. Personalities, finances, and the severity of the disease affect how people deal with their illness.

I have asked quite a few of my friends to give me some ideas of how they have learned to cope with their diseases.

My friend Ann said the most important thing for her to

learn in coping with her disease was to learn to change the subject. She found that sometimes talking about being sick made her worse. On the days when she felt she didn't want to talk about her illness, she had to plan ahead to change the subject before anyone called. She was often too sick at the time to think quick enough to change the subject once she was talking to someone.

Others may need to talk about it. It is OK to talk about it. But be sure to have other interests so you can talk about other things too.

Brenda, a friend with fibromyalgia and diabetes, says that the most important thing for her was to learn to say No.

Delphine, another friend, who has Addison's disease, agrees. She has been in the hospital four times in the past year for sodium replacement. When she overstresses physically, has respiratory problems, or vomits, her Addison's disease can go into an acute phase. Vomiting can also be an indication that she is starting into an acute phase.

Delphine said most of her family and friends know without her saying anything not to visit when they have been sick or exposed to someone vomiting. Some people have tried to tell her that it is not polite to turn away relatives who want to visit. But she says that both her counselor and her doctor have told her that she must take charge of her health. And for her, that means not having company is ill, or have been exposed to someone who is ill.

One school I attended was on the top of a hill. There was a limited number of parking spaces at the top. I knew I couldn't carry a briefcase full of books and papers up the hill from the parking lot. I had my physician fill out a form so I could get a handicap sign from the department of motor vehicles.

I never had any problems at the school or the hospital where I worked. One hot July day, I went to a department store. I knew that I would not be able to shop, walk very far in the parking lot, and drive home. I parked in a handicap space and placed the sign in the window. I noticed that the couple who had just pulled into the space beside me were whispering, but I thought nothing of it.

When I arrived back at the car, there was a note on the windshield. It read. "Don't take a handicap space. It is for handicapped people. Next time we will report you." I cried half the way home.

The next time I went to the doctor I said, "I will never use the sign away from the school or hospital again."

He looked me straight in the eyes and said, "I want you to use it all the time and use your limited energy for what you want and need. They don't see that you may have to spend the next few hours or days in bed."

When coping with a new disease, you may have to learn to pace yourself. Just this week, I was at a mall for three hours with a friend. Some of that time I was sitting. However, I spent most of the next day either in a chair or in bed.

When I just had myasthenia gravis, I could do more. I could go to school and work. I'd still have to rest but not as much as I now do with Addison's disease plus myasthenia. My doctor told me that quite often we don't know which disease is making me tired. So when we see one person coping one way with a disease and someone else coping differently, we shouldn't judge.

I have to do things differently. I can still live a rewarding life just with minor adjustments. I don't drive the car very much. Usually I have my husband or a friend take me. If a friend takes me, I always try to pay her.

Laugh when you can

You will be able to cope better if you can sometimes see the funny side of something. If you can laugh at some of your problems, they will seem easier to deal with.

Choose what to do to be hospitable

Sometimes when you have been diagnosed with an illness, you may feel useless. If you can find one small thing to do, you will feel better. Being hospitable can help you.

You may not be able to do all you have previously done. Think: Can you write letters? Can you make phone calls? Do you have a computer that you could use to send messages to others? Do you have a hobby you can do or would like to learn?

One girl in our church is in a wheelchair. She baby-sits for older children. She tells stories and helps in one of the children's divisions.

What about having people to your home? Have them help with the food too. Ask friends over for a potluck. Invite people for a time of day when you might just offer juice, tea, or a glass of water.

More and more people have food allergies. If you do, please tell your hostess. Sally, a friend of mine, cooked for her new mother-in-law. The mother in-law ate the food and didn't say anything. All of a sudden, her lips became swollen and she started to have trouble breathing. Sally said, "After that I was always scared to cook for her."

Maxine has had severe food allergies for over twelve years. When her friends go to a restaurant, she goes. She usually eats before she goes. She may order just a drink or one small thing and give it to someone else. She does not miss opportunities to be sociable. If she is invited to someone else's house, she usually takes one dish she can eat. If people notice she is eating differently, she just tells them she has food allergies.

Erma cannot help do the dishes when she goes to someone's home. One of her hostesses said, "Never mind, you'll get to do dishes the first 100 years in heaven."

It is important for your friends and family to know your situation. If you have invited them over and on the day they are supposed to come you can't have them, tell them you can't have them. Don't make yourself sicker by pushing beyond your limits. This is also true in the reverse. If they have asked you over and you can't go, say so.

Sometimes others may not understand no matter what you say or do. You may feel like praying, "Lord, help them to be sick for a while so they will know how it feels."

You can be hospitable no matter what chronic disease or handicap you have.

Dear Lord:
Help me to find something I can do to help another.

CHAPTER FIFTEEN

Hospitality Helpers

*Y*ou can be more hospitable and have fun doing it by applying the following principles, which I call hospitality helpers:

- I will try to spend some time each day in private devotions.
- I understand that I don't have to do everything perfectly.
- I will be myself and not compare myself to someone else.
- I will not overstress or overspend in energy, time, or money.
- I will put my health before hospitality.
- I will do what "fits" my personality.

◉ I will remember to be more concerned with people than things.

◉ I will be hospitable to myself and choose one thing each day to brighten my life—listen to the birds sing, read a funny book, smell a flower, look for the rainbow.

◉ I know that Jesus loves me no matter what!

Happy Hospitality!

I Asked You Home, and . . .

I asked you home,
You didn't care,
A can of beans
You had to share.

What about the dishes
In my sink?
When you saw them,
What did you think?

You laughed and said,
"I'm just like you.

I've got dishes
In my sink too.

My bed's not made
If the truth be told.
I'm struggling too
In a survival mode."

A brand new friend
I found today
When I didn't let
Pride stand in my way.